THE ENERGY SELF-DEFENSE SERIES - No. 3

ANNI & CARSTEN SENNOV

ENERGY
SELF-DEFENSE
for
YOUNG ADULTS

good adventures publishing

Energy Self-Defense for Young Adults

©2017, Anni & Carsten Sennov and Good Adventures Publishing
First edition, first impression
Set with Cambria
Layout: Anni Sennov – www.sennovpartners.com
Cover design: Michael Bernth – www.monovoce.dk
Author photo: Aamod & Sophelia Korhonen - www.balanceisjoy.com

Original title in Danish:
"Tag din kraft tilbage nu!"
Original title in English:
"Get Your Power Back Now!"
Translated into English by: Sue Jonas Dupuis

ISBN 978-87-7206-002-6

Contents

Notice

When reading this book please be in a spirit of open-mindedness.

Although the authors and the publisher have made every effort to ensure the accuracy and completeness of information contained in this book, we assume no responsibility for errors, inaccuracies, omissions, or any inconsistencies herein. Any offense caused to people, places, or organizations is unintentional.

Readers should use their own judgment, or consult a holistic medical expert or their personal physician for specific applications to their individual problems.

Welcome!

Most of you young people are very clear in the way you express yourselves compared to others, both when you speak and when you use body language and your energy without actually having to say anything. Often one doesn't have to know you at all to know what you think about things. It's so obvious just by looking at you to know whether you are interested in something, or completely indifferent to or bored by it, or if you are happy, angry or sad.

When you are very direct, as many of you are, then it should be really easy for most adults to communicate with you. Unfortunately not all adults are as direct and honest in the way they express themselves as you are. They aren't always completely honest with themselves. All too often they don't dare to look the truth in the eye and accept life as it is. Therefore it can be extremely provocative for them to have you stand up and tell them that it isn't really so difficult to decide to do something to change the situation. It is interesting that young people and children are often quicker to realize that there is something wrong in their parents' relationships than the parents themselves. So often, they are not surprised when their parents end up getting a divorce.

With your direct way of being you must unfortunately be prepared for the roles sometimes being reversed, meaning that you behave in a more adult, responsible and insightful way than some adults. Maybe you actually end up giving the adults good advice, and it is of course wonderful that young people and adults can support each other. However, as a young person you must not forget who has lived the longest, and therefore who has had the most experience of life. Just imagine if adults did not share their life experience with you, then all young people and children throughout the world would have to make the very same mistakes as they did in the olden days and we would perhaps still be living in caves. Worst of all, they would probably not have developed the computers, cell phones or iPads that many of you spend so much time on every day.

This is the reason that we decided to write this Energy Self-Defense guide, to share a certain type of knowledge with you that not many parents and adults are able to explain, either to themselves or to you. As authors of this book, energy is our greatest interest and because we work with it every day, it makes it easy for us to explain how it works for others.

In this energy guide you will learn what happens on an invisible level between people when there could be a problem between you and those you love most, as well as with other people you may encounter in your daily lives. So when things sometimes look really difficult, it could in fact just take a simple thing to change the situation, if only you knew what to do and how.

So if you are interested in learning how you can master your own energy when you are with other people and if you sometimes feel lonely, then you have picked up the right book and we have tried to make it as short, simple and easy to understand as possible.

Happy reading!

Anni & Carsten Sennov

Young people and children know about energy

As a young person, it is generally much easier for you than it is for your parents to understand energy. It is often faster and more effective to use your own power and strength to deal with energy than if your parents had to control your energy for you. The fact is that many of you are born with an increased and much stronger personal energy and have a more developed understanding of the energy-related and technological developments taking place on earth right now than your parents do.

You are the adults of the future and therefore you have an energy within you that will extend a little further out into the future than your parents' energy. Your parents' energy, in turn, is supposed to be used at this particular moment in time so that they can advise and guide you young people, so that you can become good citizens of the world.

Now is the time to begin sorting out your energy, beginning each morning, at lunchtime and at night, as well as after you have been with other people at school, at work or at home. This is what our four children have been doing for years, and now that three of them are adults and have left home, they still sort out their energy. In fact it is as natural for them to keep an eye on their energy as it is to brush their teeth or to eat and sleep.

Exchange of energy

There are three types of energy exchanges between people, and if you are always aware of which of these three types are operating when you are with others, then you will quickly be a master at balancing your own energy and coping well when you are interacting with others.

You may be in perfect balance in your relationship with some people because you support and help each other equally and want to do good things for each other, thus keeping both of you happy.

Or you might also choose to volunteer to help others just because you want to do something nice for them, and because it makes you happy to do it. They may not have the energy to help you in return or to give you anything back, but you feel great because they are people that you like and they are happy that you are helping them.

And finally there are the energy thieves – people who want something from you, and who are unhappy no matter how much you help them or give them. In fact, spending time with them and trying to help them will put you in a bad mood. Maybe they will even take something from you without permission, and then you will be in an extremely bad mood. So stay far away from them.

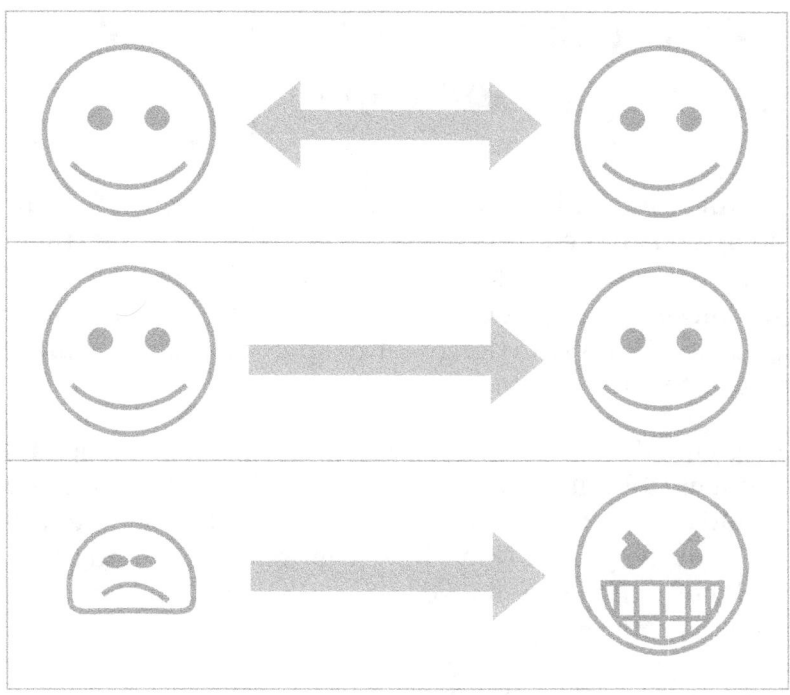

Do you think about other people too much?

Maybe you think about a good friend or a girlfriend or boyfriend all the time, either because you really like them or because you want to help them and worry about them. If so, you risk giving them too much attention. This increases their energy level so that other people will find them more interesting to be with.

By giving them too much attention, the result may be that suddenly they don't have as much time to be with you as you would really like. This is because if you think about them all the time, they will always have your energy around them, and they will then not need to be with you as much to have some of your energy.

You could say that they are living so well on the attention that you are giving them; it's as if they don't really feel that they are missing you. As humans we usually only miss those who matter to us if they aren't around and we can't feel their energy because they are busy with something else.

So the result of giving your best friends and/or your girl-friend or boyfriend or other people a lot of attention by thinking about them all the time, especially when you're apart, is that often, they go around with twice as much energy and attractiveness. This happens without them even realizing it, while you are sitting at home waiting to hear from them and feeling completely forgotten and empty inside. This is because your own energy and attention has been laid on top of their energy as an extra-strong energy field, so they suddenly seem much more appealing and interesting than they might actually be.

Try to think back, as you have probably experienced this more than once.

Most of us would really like to be around people with strong charisma and lots of energy to share, and of course it is okay for energy-rich people to go around with their own charisma and attractiveness. However, it's definitely not okay if they go around with both their own energy and your energy too. In the meantime, you may feel powerless and forgotten, while they are using your energy to have fun and live life to the fullest.

If they go around with both their own energy and yours, they can attract a lot of additional benefits and extra attention that would otherwise have been split between them and you, and other people will not know that some of their attraction energy actually comes from you. People who are energy-rich are able to attract the benefits and attention which are really for two people, and though you have been supporting them with all your attention, you will probably not get any benefit from the relationship.

In good friendships and relationships there needs to be a balance between the two sides. You should always keep your energy with you and let others benefit from it when they are with you. If you are a nice, fun and loving person, others will want to be with you, and you can control when you are together, so you don't always have to wait for when it suits them to be with you.

How to help your friends

Perhaps you want to help a really good friend and/or a girl-friend or boyfriend or a family member in a certain situation. Then you have probably already guessed that by thinking about them a lot and sending them good thoughts, you can help them to succeed in an amazing way. The abundance of the energy you give to them will benefit them if they have exams or are playing in an important football game, or if they are in the hospital, and so on.

After their exams or football game, it is important that you remember to draw all your energy back towards yourself. If this is not done, others will still have your energy available to them, which they can use as they please, and that is perhaps not the way you would use the energy yourself.

Unpleasant and annoying people

If you go around thinking a lot about people who are unpleasant or do ugly and hateful things to others, they will get a lot of extra attention and energy from you that they do not deserve to have. This thinking could also allow you to build up fears about what they might do.

Unfortunately, thinking about someone or something bad all the time can lead to attracting bad experiences and unpleasant people into your life. Because you have given these negative thoughts your energy, suddenly the things you feared the most could happen.

It's like when you are afraid to walk alone in the dark after watching a scary movie, because you are then giving all your power and energy to the darkness and to things you can't see.

If instead you imagined that you were watching the movie without sound, then all of a sudden it wouldn't seem so scary, and it would be much easier for you to hold on to your energy and get rid of your fear, which is actually just energy expressed in a non-productive way, so that nothing and nobody else can control it.

You can do the same with unpleasant and annoying people, and instead of listening to all their negative talk, you can begin to think about something positive, and then they will have no power over you and your energy.

Many young people often make trouble just to get attention, simply because they are bored and may not get enough attention and love at home, or because there are problems at home. Often these troublemakers are just lonely and neglected young people who are trying to get attention. There is rarely anything malicious about them. So if you occasionally show them a little care and respect by talking to them and telling them in a positive way that you don't like the things they are doing, they will usually stop being so annoying.

However, it is not just young people who can be annoying to others around them and create a lot of turmoil. Adults can be like that too, especially if they are not being intellectually challenged, or because they do not have something exciting to do at work or in their free time. People like this can be a nightmare to work with if you are an adult.

At school it is of course the responsibility of the teachers to control annoying students, but the class can also get involved in solving the problem. In this case it will help if you choose to draw all your energy back from your annoying classmates, otherwise there is a risk that they will fill the classroom with their anxiety and frustration and this will damage both your concentration and your learning opportunities.

It doesn't actually make any difference whether you give other people positive or negative attention, or whether you send them good or bad thoughts, because thoughts are energy and can act just like fuel for a car. The more fuel or attention you fill them with, the longer they can run and the more damage they can do if they aren't in balance. So it is much better to totally ignore unpleasant and annoying people, just as you should avoid watching horror movies if they make you scared.

If you have no choice and cannot keep away from them, you can attempt to forget that they are around you and try your best to ignore them. This avoids them picking you as a possible victim for their nastiness and teasing.

What you should do

The following exercise will allow you to master your own energy, only takes two minutes a day to do, and you can do it anytime, anywhere.

First, imagine in your mind's eye that you are sending everyone else's energy back to them and you are drawing all your own energy back to yourself.

Now say the following sentence out loud or to yourself, or see it in your mind's eye, and if you can't see it in your mind's eye, just repeat the sentence as many times as you can or have time for. It is better to do it twice in one day than not to do it at all:

> *"I am now drawing*
> *all my personal energy back to myself*
> *in a completely purified form,*
> *from all people, places and situations,*
> *and I am now sending everyone else's energy*
> *out of my energy field and back to them*
> *in the same form as they originally sent it to me."*

The more often you do this, the better you will be at holding on to your own energy. So if you do it at least in the morning, at lunchtime and at night, and also when you have been with your friends and family or at school, work or at a party, then you are well on the way to doing yourself a lot of good.

A bad start to the day

Everyone, whether they are young people, children or adults, has the experience, once in a while, of starting the day in a really awful way. Maybe you are tired and grumpy in the morning because you have slept badly or because you have been thinking about something that annoys you.

When you get to school or work, everything continues to be really unpleasant, because others can read your thoughts and feelings very clearly, whether you think it's possible or not.

Some people can sense your grumpiness and others can see immediately that you are in a bad mood, even if you are trying to hide it. Most happy people will keep themselves away from you until you are in a better mood. Other people who get a kick out of conflict and trouble will be happy to get close to you because they can sense that they might have the chance to sneak some extra energy from you because you are tired and in a bad mood and can't keep proper control of your own energy.

So if are you tired, irritated or grumpy, think this thought as many times as you can:

"I am happy and everything good is coming to me."

This will stop you from attracting negative attention from others, whether it's at school, during sports, at work or at home. This will also stop you from getting into trouble or from hurting yourself, just because you are in a slightly worse mood than usual and are therefore not as aware of what is happening around you as you normally are.

Do you give too much of yourself to others?

You can't love too much. However, in your desire to help others you may totally overwhelm them with your love, attention, and help. This is because they cannot contain as much attention and care at one time as you can.

Because they don't have nearly as much energy as you, their energy reservoir may be much smaller than yours. Therefore, there may be flooding everywhere if you try to help them by filling their reservoir with extra energy. This might be true even if they have asked you for help themselves. Sometimes people may get angry even when you have just helped them the best you could, because they simply can't contain the large amount of energy and power that you have given them.

If you are a person with lots of energy, in order to avoid over-filling other people with your excess energy, you may find that you burn your energy best through sports, hobbies, and other activities that you really love. By doing a sport or something else that you are really interested in, you should attempt to split up your excess energy amongst as many different people as possible during the day and the week. Also, remember to always draw all your energy and attention back to yourself when you are no longer with others, and never give your friends and family, even your parents, more attention than they can tolerate. Also be aware that you have to experiment to find out how much attention other people can bear to have from you, without it becoming so strong that they can't handle it. You will get tips about how to do this in the chapter *How to do it*.

How to do it

It is easy enough to see or hear whether other people are getting angry because you are trying to help them more than they can bear, as they will constantly complain and be deeply dissatisfied, or else they will become mean and sarcastic.

When it comes to certain people who would like to have more of your energy, you may notice that they start to behave in a different way than they normally would. If they suddenly start to become extraordinarily successful and completely forget about you, then it's worth drawing all your energy back to yourself and sending all their energy back to them.

It may also be that they start to change their behavior just by being near you, and this can sometimes be clearly seen by the fact that some people become very self-absorbed and start talking at a very loud volume, while others may suddenly be able to do many things that they wouldn't normally be able to do.

Extra energy, which does not really belong to the person, can show itself in many ways. Notice, for example, whether the person suddenly starts doing extraordinary things which they wouldn't be able to do normally and feel whether it is actually your energy that they are running on. If it is your energy that is being used, then you must immediately start to draw all your energy back as we described in the chapter *What you should do.*

Imagine in your mind's eye that you draw all your personal energy back to yourself by saying the following mantra:

"I am now drawing
all my personal energy back to myself
in a completely purified form,
from all people, places and situations,
and I am now sending everyone else's energy
out of my energy field and back to them
in the same form as they originally sent it to me."

Are you easily influenced by others?

If you are very sensitive it can be hard for you to be with other people who are harsh and negative. If you don't take extra care to protect your energy so that their thoughts and unpleasant ways of speaking don't affect you, then you could easily end up with unwanted and negative feelings, even when these negative people are no longer near you.

Maybe you have already tried to send all their bad thoughts and negative energy back to them and it hasn't worked properly. Instead, you could try to transform their negative energy into positive energy that can benefit you.

As an important ground rule when working with Energy Self-Defense, remember that you must never open yourself up to let other people's bad energy come into your energy field, where it can disturb your personal balance in order to get access to your energy. However, if someone's negative energy is floating everywhere in the air around you, and they don't want to have anything to do with their own bad energy, then you are within your rights to convert all of this energy into something positive that will benefit you.

Imagine in your mind's eye that all the bad energy that others are sending in your direction or that they are filling the room with is changing from being negative and dark to being positive, bright and happy, so that it is you who is benefitting from it. Also, imagine how the positive energy is settling around you and acting as extra strength and creating a more powerful energy field for you.

In fact it is so easy that you'll find it difficult to believe, but the best thing is that it actually works!

Learn to stand
on your own two feet

If there is something you really want, things can often succeed more easily if there are a number of you working together. For example, you have a much greater chance of winning a football game if everyone on the team can agree to tackle each play together.

On the other hand, it is a sign of weakness to get together in a group to bully and bother someone who is not in the group. If the individual members of the group can't stand alone in relation to the person who is outside the group, who's really the weakest?

All young people are rehearsing, each in their own way, to become adults. When you are an adult you should be able to manage yourself and stand on your own two feet. After all, you can't take your friends with you to work every day. As you are learning how to do this, you will come to know how to entertain yourself. So it's best that you don't get too bored in your own company, as then you risk boring others when you are with them.

It is also really important for you to have some good friends who don't share exactly the same views and who don't have the same upbringing as you. It can teach you how to work well with people who live and think in a different way from you.

As you are preparing to stand on your own two feet, remember that all people are different and unique in their own way. In fact it would be really boring if everyone behaved in exactly the same way. It is all these differences that help to make our lives exciting and challenging, and so it is important for you to find the strength, both in yourself and in your relationships with other people, to be who you really are.

People will like you for who you are. Don't try to be someone you're not.

You may find yourself imitating your friends because you think they are smarter or tougher than you feel you are inside. Perhaps they are only being tough because they want to make an impression on other people, including you. When you are relaxed and being yourself, your friends will be able to feel that you are completely honest and that you can be trusted. So then they can easily be themselves when they are with you, without constantly having to think about what you might say about them afterwards to other people.

Deep down everyone would prefer to be popular by being themselves completely and utterly, instead of pretending that they are a different person from the one they really are.

Do you have too little energy?

If you are completely out of energy, think about what you've done, where you've been and who you've been with.

Here are a few tips if you feel out of energy after sitting in front of the computer all day. Go outside and get some fresh air, drink lots of water, exercise, dance a little, or go for a run.

When you sit for a long time in front of the computer or the TV, or you have your cell phone and your iPad on your lap, then you are exposing yourself to radiation which is definitely not good for your body and your brain. Try to sleep as far away as you can from your computer, cell phone or other electronic equipment. That way you will get a better and more refreshing night's sleep. Talk to your parents, friends, industry experts, etc. about what types of protection you can use to reduce the radiation from all these devices you have at home, as there are many options available on the market today.

If you have ever slept outdoors, then you know that you generally feel much more refreshed because of the fresh air, and also due to the fact that you are sleeping well away from the radiation coming from your computer and cell phone, etc.

If you get tired or irritable from being in certain places, it may be because some unpleasant things have happened there, and the energy from those events is still hanging in the air and affecting you. As much as possible, avoid going to these places again, as it is not your job to clean up other people's bad energy.

If, however, your tiredness is due to being with energy

thieves, read about how to handle this situation in the chapter titled *What you should do*, earlier in this book.

Do you have too much energy?

If you have an extraordinarily large amount of energy, you can share your surplus energy with others as we wrote about in the chapter *How to help your friends*. However, always remember to draw your energy back to you once they have had enough to get them through a particular situation. Secondly, remember to draw all your energy back to yourself if you can clearly see and feel that they can't bear to receive more without becoming very focused on themselves.

If there is a balance between your energy and your friends' energy, and both or all of you have lots of excess energy, then there is no point in giving energy to each other. Instead, find something positive to use your excess energy on which can benefit others who maybe need a helping hand. There are always plenty of people you can help if you want to. It's important, though, that you use your surplus energy on something that you're comfortable with. Otherwise you run the risk that your joy in helping others will soon disappear.

If you have so much energy that you can't control it, and it is expressed in an inappropriate way, then we would recommend that you put extra focus on first drawing all your energy back to you from the people, places and situations where you have used your energy inappropriately. Always remember to clean the energy before bringing it back. You can do that by imagining that you are running the energy through a cleansing filter before you let it come into your energy field. Then take a few deep breaths, preferably outdoors in the fresh air.

Finally, you then have to decide what you want to use all your energy on by trying to feel deep down if there is something you are passionate about and which you would like to use a lot of energy on.

Maybe you want to learn to play an instrument, to act, or do hip hop? Or maybe you're crazy about motorcross riding and want to feel the speed and excitement under your skin? It might also be that you are passionate about helping other people even if you aren't an adult yet. Who says you have to be an adult to start something big in life? Today it's so simple to spread your message to the whole world via the internet if you have a good idea or something really interesting you want to share with others, or if you sing like an angel. All you have to do is record a video of yourself or others on your cell phone and upload it on YouTube. If you say or do something amazing you will get lots of positive feedback.

It may be the case that you can't figure out how to express your energy in a sensible and balanced way when you are with other people, but that doesn't mean that you have a lot of bad energy in you. It means instead that you just don't know how to handle your own energy, and you need help and guidance to change the situation. We hope this energy guide can help, and if you're struggling, we recommend that you have a chat with some adults to see if they have some good ideas on how you can start using your energy in a positive and satisfying way. Talk to your parents, but also to other adults such as your teachers, grandparents, your friends' parents or your neighbors and colleagues at work, as it can often be interesting and instructive to hear what they have to say. They will certainly have lived their lives differently from your parents, and have unique life experiences to share that are exactly what you may need to move forward in your life in a positive way.

Always clean up after yourself when you leave

To be polite and respectful of other people, you should always clean up your energy and take it with you when you leave. This applies to when you leave other people's homes, and also when you have been to sports practice, in school or at work so you do not just fly out of the door without checking whether you have everything with you.

You can compare it to being a good and attentive guest who will always help to clear the table when visiting other people, or disposing of your popcorn and drink when leaving the movie theatre for example.

Keeping control of your energy when you are with other people means that it will be easier for you to keep your daily energy account in balance, so nobody else will have to do things for you.

Thanks for your time

We believe it is every parent's responsibility to ensure that young people understand and experience how things are connected in the real world. This depends, of course, on how much knowledge your parents have about these things. Obviously, however, their main task in life is to guide you in living your life in the best way possible, and to help you to find suitable solutions to the problems that you run up against during your formative years. After all, it is they who chose to put you in the world.

On the other hand, we know that not many parents or other adults have such deep insight into the energy connections as we have described them in this Energy Self-Defense guide. In case you still live at home, we highly recommend that you share the things you have read in this book with your parents. We have also written Energy Self-Defense guides for Women, for Men, and for Parents, so you can share your experiences with each other.

Lastly, please don't keep this energy knowledge to yourself. Share this book with your friends so that they may know the secret to your happiness !!!

Many thanks for reading this Energy Self-Defense guide :o)

And what now?

Start using the knowledge you have gained here in your everyday life. Even though you may have a little trouble remembering it at first, gradually it will become quite natural for you to sort out your energy. It can actually reach the point that you become annoyed with yourself if you forget to do it, because it often leads to some stupid problems which could easily have been avoided. So **always** remember to sort your energy!

And if you would like, feel free to help others acquire the same knowledge and insight that you have now, by giving this energy guide as a different kind of gift to a good friend, or to your girlfriend or boyfriend, or to a family member. The more people around you who know about energy sorting, the better it will be for everyone.

If you are curious and would like to know more, please feel free to look at our websites to see what other interesting books and articles we have written.

We also organize courses, which you and your parents would certainly enjoy taking part in.

www.energyselfdefense.com
(Energy Self-Defense guides & online courses)

www.sennovpartners.com

www.annisennov.com (books, articles, etc.)

www.carstensennov.com (management consulting)

www.fourelementprofile.com (courses)

www.good-adventures.com (publishing)

We also recommend that you read this book

The Little Energy Guide 1
Take care of your own energy

Anni & Carsten Sennov

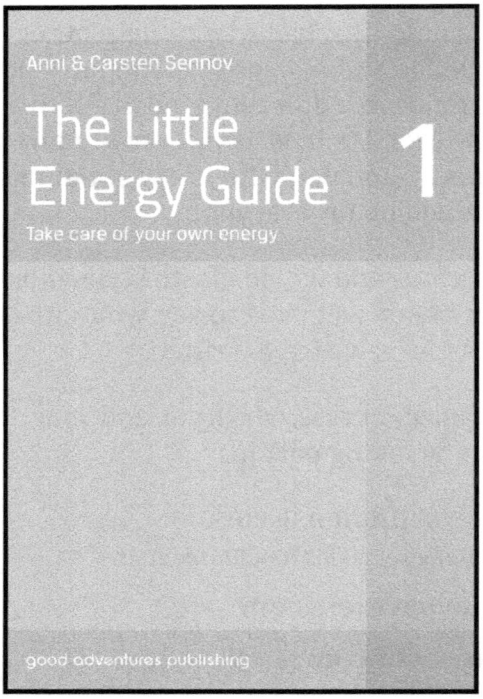

To rip out and hang on your wall, mirror, etc. $\rightarrow$ $\rightarrow$ $\rightarrow$

Energy Self-Defense for Young Adults

Energy Self-Defense Mantra

*"I am now drawing
all my personal energy
back to myself
in a completely purified form,
from all people, places
and situations,
and I am now sending
everyone else's energy
out of my energy field
and back to them
in the same form
as they originally sent it to me."*

Energy Self-Defense for Young Adults